TAKING CARE OF EARTH

Written By: Anna DiGilio

All rights reserved. No part of this publication may be reproduced, distributed, or transmitted in any form or by any means, including photocopying, recording, or other electronic or mechanical methods, without the prior written permission of the publisher, except in the case of brief quotations embodied in critical reviews and certain other noncommercial uses permitted by copyright law.

For permission requests, write to the publisher:
Laprea Publishing
info@lapreapublishing.com

Website: www.GuidedReaders.com

ISBN: 978-1-64579-153-9

© 2018 Anna DiGilio

Photo Credits:
Cover, Title Page, 6 (top): Adobe Stock; Sunny studio. 3: Depositphotos; AntonMatyukha. 4 (top), 11 (bottom): Depositphotos; ArturVerkhovetskiy. 4 (bottom): Depositphotos; Patryk_Kosmider. 5: Depositphotos; Derejeb. 6 (bottom left): Depositphotos; Ivaleks. 6 (bottom right): Depositphotos; Pashabo. 7, 8 (bottom left), 9 (bottom right), 11 (top): Shutterstock; Wavebreakmedia. 8 (top): Adobe Stock; Oneinchpunch. 8 (bottom right): Depositphotos; Alfa4studio. 9 (top): Adobe Stock; DragonImages. 9 (bottom left): Depositphotos; Littleny. 10 (top): Adobe Stock; VanderWolf Images. 10 (bottom): Adobe Stock; Rob245. 12: Depositphotos; Cozyta. 13 (top): Depositphotos; Rawpixel. 13 (bottom left): Adobe Stock; Auremar. 13 (bottom right): Depositphotos; Andreus. 14 (top): Adobe Stock; JJAVA. 14 (bottom left, bottom right): Depositphotos; Opicobello.

TABLE OF CONTENTS

Our Amazing Home.................................Page 4

Earth Day ....Page 7

Arbor Day ....Page 9

Helping Earth Every Day ....Page 10

How Else Can We Help?..........................Page 14

Glossary...Page 15

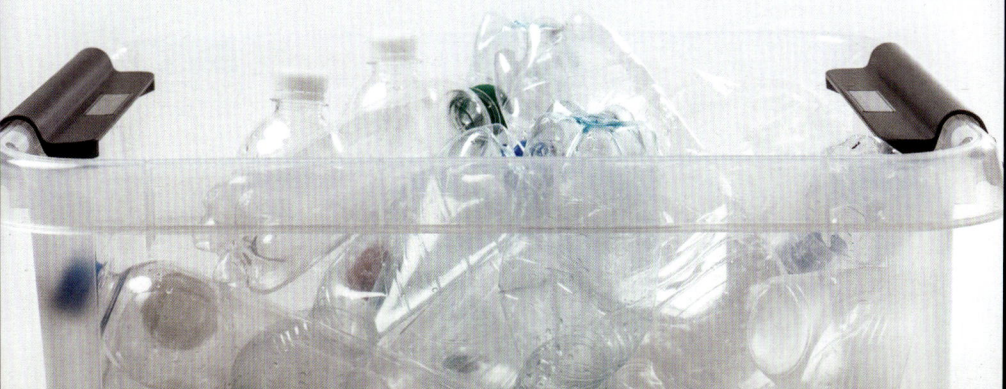

Our Amazing Home

Earth is our home. It has living things and nonliving things. Together, they make Earth a good home.

Earth needs our help to keep being a good home. We can't just move away if it gets too dirty. There's nowhere else to go!

Many more people now live on Earth than long ago. We use more than our fair share of the space.

Other living things have a <u>right</u> to live, too. Also, we need them so we can stay alive. If they die out, all of Earth is in trouble.

The streets of New York City are busy.

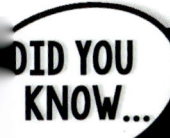

DID YOU KNOW... Bees carry special plant powder from flower to flower. The powder helps fruit and vegetable plants grow. What will happen to our food if bees die out?

We need Earth's help to stay alive, and so do other living things. We all need clean air, clean water, and clean food.

Earth needs our help so it can keep giving us these things. How can we help?

Earth Day

Earth Day is a special day to think about how to help Earth. It's also a day to DO things to help Earth.

Many people go to <u>nature</u> places on Earth Day. In nature, it's easy to <u>remember</u> why taking care of our world is important.

People around the world honor Earth Day each year on April 22.

Earth Day is also a day to take care of nature. There are many ways to help.

On Earth Day, people also learn how to take care of Earth every day. Later in this book, you'll read about some of those ways.

Working with other people to help Earth is fun!

Arbor Day

Arbor Day is a special day to honor trees. People plant trees and take care of trees.

Trees make oxygen gas. People and other animals need oxygen so we can breathe. Trees are important for many other reasons, too.

Helping Earth Every Day

Earth needs our help every day. People use a lot of <u>energy</u> at home, work, and school. We use gas in our cars. We also buy a lot of things. All these things create <u>waste</u>. Waste makes land, air, and oceans dirty. What can we do about these problems?

Burning coal to make electricity makes the air dirty.

Landfills are huge piles of waste.

We can reduce waste, which means making less of it. Every time people make a new <u>product</u>, it makes waste. If we buy less things, we make less waste.

Instead of buying a book at the book store or on Amazon, you can borrow it from the library and return it when you are done. You are reusing books.

We could reuse things. If we do need something, we can often get it used. First, someone else uses it. Then, we reuse it—we use it again. Or maybe we use it first and then give it to someone else.

The scrap yard will reuse the metal by melting it and turning it into a new product.

Reducing and reusing both save money and help the earth.

Another way we can help is to recycle. When we recycle, <u>materials</u> get used again. Then they do not become waste. Recycling helps Earth stay cleaner.

Glass, plastic, paper, and cardboard can be recycled.

How Else Can We Help?

When we help Earth, we also help ourselves and all living things. There are hundreds of ways to help. Here are a few:
- Use cloth bags.
- Turn off lights and water.
- Grow a garden!

How do you want to help Earth?

GLOSSARY

<u>energy</u>
power from electricity, heat, or other sources

<u>materials</u>
matter that can be used to make things

<u>nature</u>
the world around us, which includes plants, animals, land, and oceans

<u>product</u>
something that is made or grown to be sold or used

GLOSSARY

<u>remember</u>
to think of something again

<u>right</u>
a freedom or power that a living thing deserves to have

<u>waste</u>
something that is unwanted, thrown away, or left over and useless